SECTION 8

Written by
TJ Sykes

Illustrated by
Webster Quoc Nguyen

Copyright © 2018 TJ Sykes

All Rights Reserved
This book may not be reproduced in whole or in part, by any means now known or yet to be invented, without the express written permission of the Copyright Owner, excepting brief quotes used in reviews or scholarly journals. The purchase of a copy of this book does not confer upon the purchaser license to use this work or any part therein in other works, including derivatives.

First Edition: 2018

ISBN #: 978-0-578-43516-9

TJ Sykes
Richmond, California
USA

I dedicate this book to:

Carolyn Marie

Latina Marie Brown-Sykes
Sunrise: July 6,1966- Sunset: October 3, 2002

Camaron Perry Walker
Sunrise: February 22, 1991- Sunset: June 14th, 2006

Carmel
Sunrise: October 6, 1952 -Sunset: February 9, 2009

Demaria Corgile
Sunrise: March 6,1978- Sunset: December 21, 2012

Fontino Hardy Jr
Sunrise: April 22, 1986- Sunset: July 14, 2015

Khalil Foster
Sunrise: March 23,1999- Sunset: November 23, 2017

Kevin Drac Williams
Sunrise: August 3,1965- Sunset: January 6,2018

Javoni Foster
Sunrise: July 31,1997- Sunset: April 7, 2018

May they all Live on Through Me.

FOREWORD

Walking upon our streets in Richmond California we see ghosts. A collage of tattooed memories spin around scarred minds like dice games and chrome 26's on cocaine foreign cars black boys gamble their life for. No matter where you stand, there is a cypher of dead homies that crowd the entrance of corner stores where liquored spilled over mama tears for baby boys dying to be men. Listen with your heart, and you'll hear the rocks cry out. Front lawns cough blood onto the sidewalks that stain between bottom crease on our fresh J's. The price for our freedom is death. The government call places like this low-income, project housing apartment complex, townhouses or section 8. For beautiful brothers like Tj, this is home.

Tj Sykes captures his community vividly when he speaks. His writing is always honest and hard hitting like the uppercuts from poverty's fist. He walks you through the path young women and men take everyday when juking through the obstacles that awaits the stumbling feet of the idle mind. Tj is a voice that represents the coping process from whistling of bullets through playgrounds, spilling the young life blood that inks the pages of his poetry notebook. Tj invite's you to listen with your heart and hear us all with your eyes. Because of this brother, our people will be seen.

Donte Clark
Richmond, California

Introduction

I go by Tj Sykes. My full name is Ty'John Sykes. I am a Richmond, California native. I grew up in Kennedy Manor. I spent most of my elementary school years living in East Oakland. I have three siblings, two brothers, one sister, and a host of brothers and sisters sent to me by the Most High. This book started off as a poem based off my 20 years experience living in section 8 housing. This is the first book I've ever written.

The purpose of this poem is to share my lived experiences with the world, sparking the minds of the readers to express their lived experiences in which ever artistic medium they choose. The idea of creating this book came from two of my co-workers at the time, Francisco Rojas and Webster Nguyen. Included are some of the struggles my family and I faced. The pictures included depict the things I saw first hand, intertwined with my imagination. The images you will see are people I know personally, mostly close relatives.

As a people, I feel it is important that we not only share our lived experiences but also imagine ourselves outside of the conditions we were placed in. I hope you enjoy this book.

SECTION 8

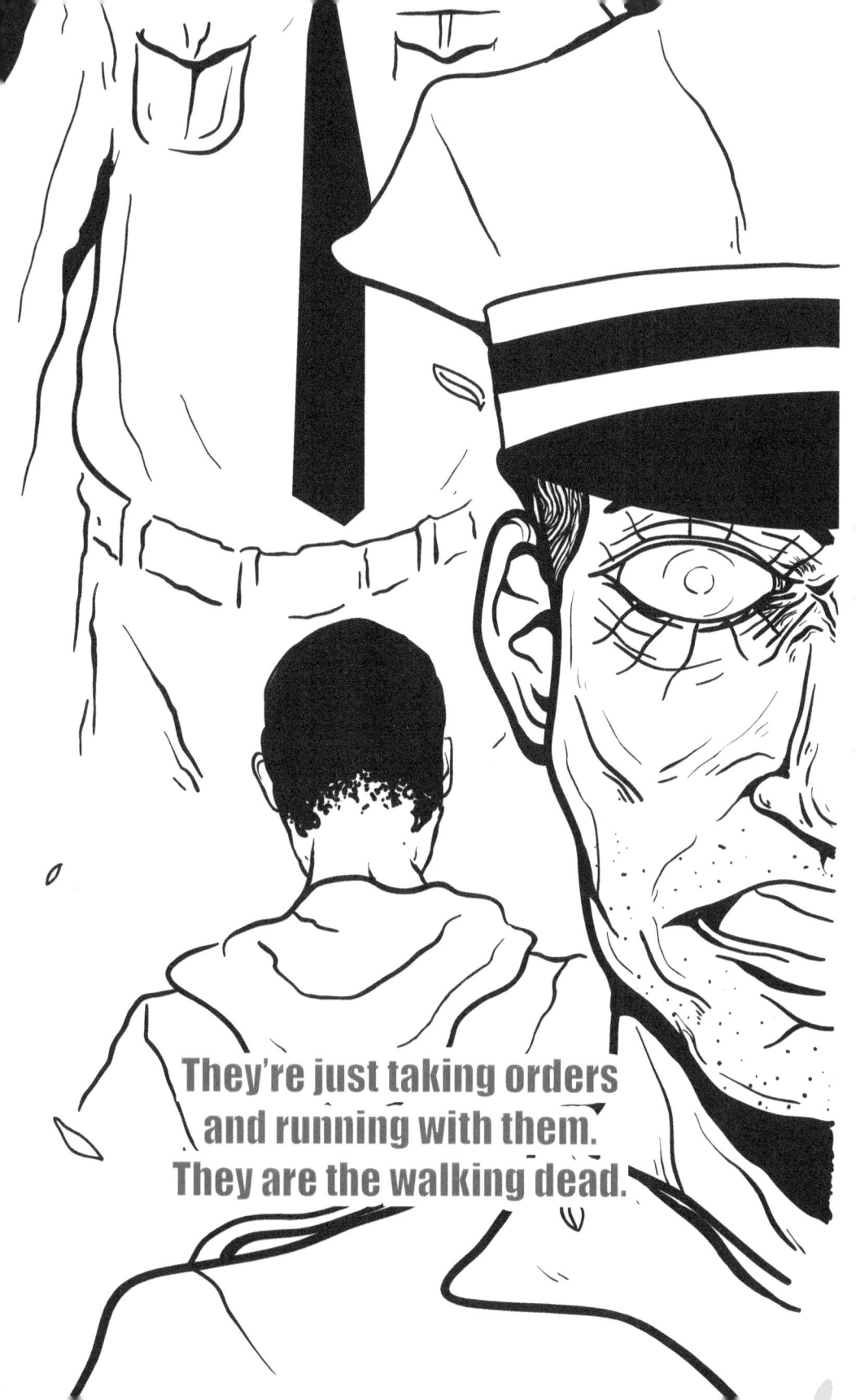

Section 8 where my people are woke up at 6:30 a.m. by the loud motor of a leaf blower, blowing leaves from one side to another only to collect and throw them in the trash interrupting the natural process.

Section 8 broken and outdated stoves and refrigerators.

Residents don't even know the management, how could we call this a community. I call it imprisonment.

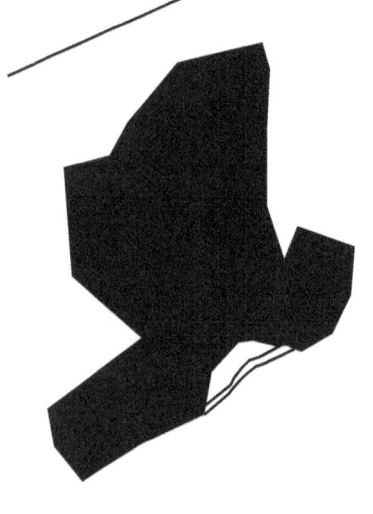

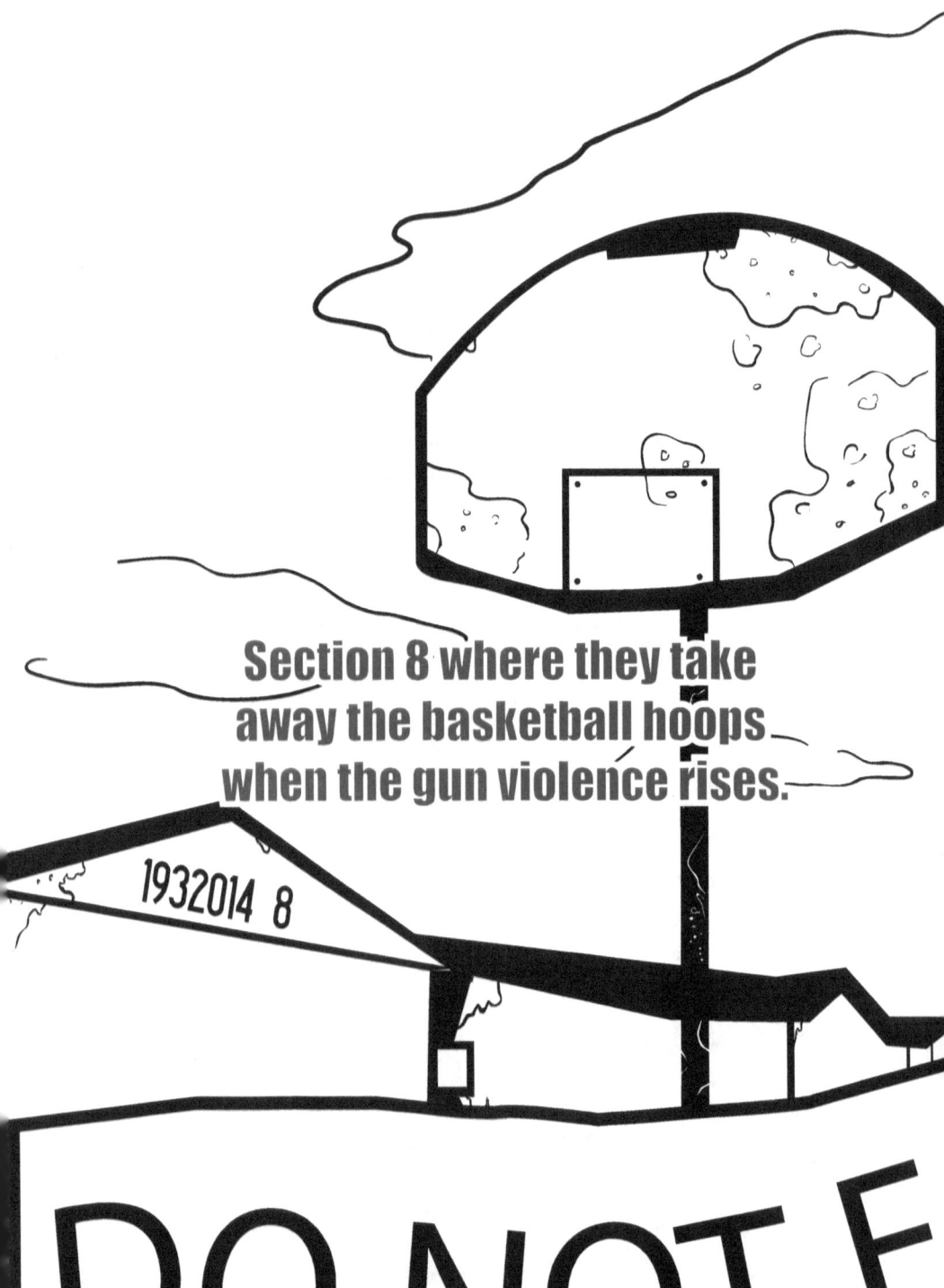

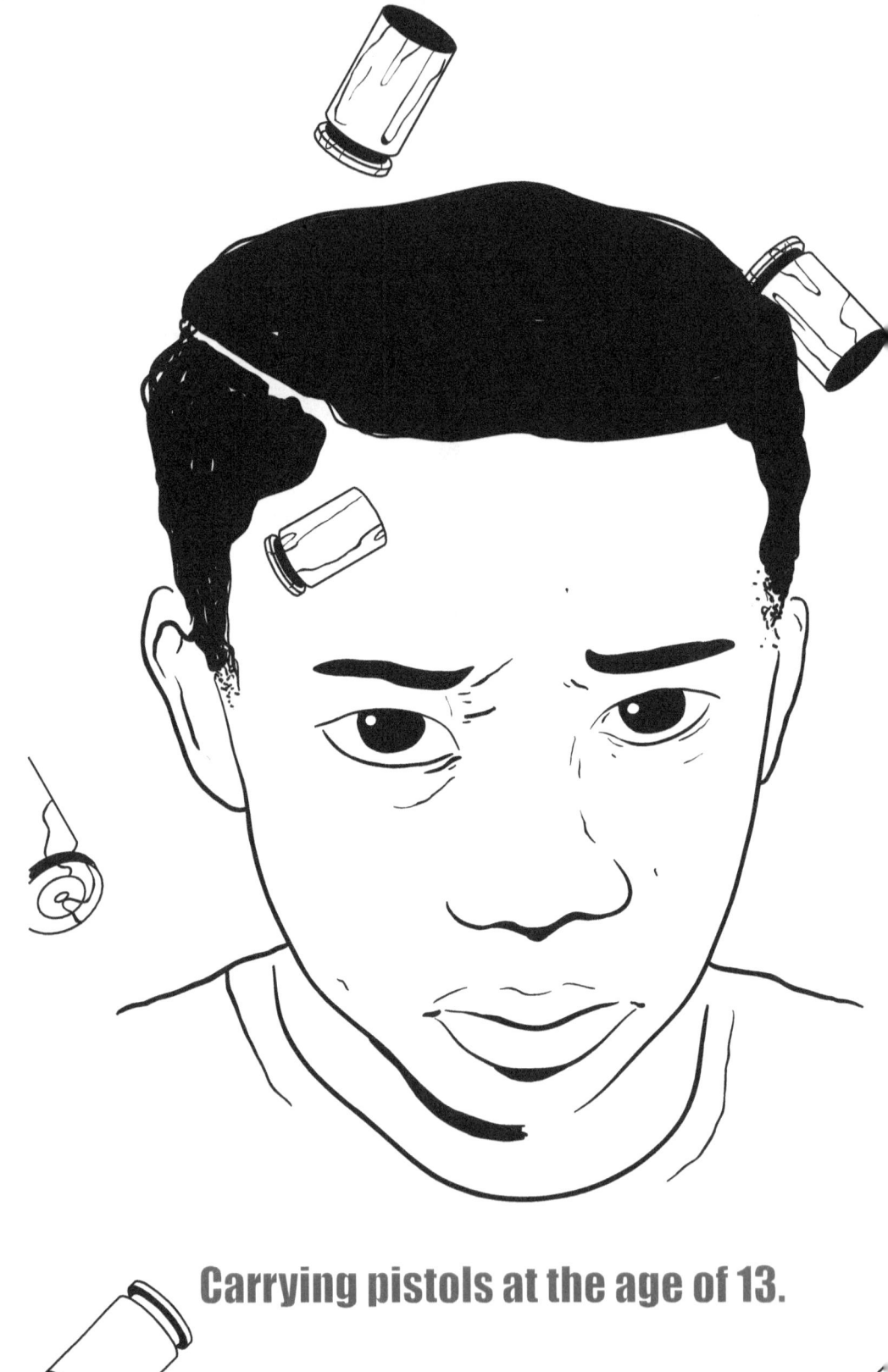

m that section 8 boy who has so much bottled up pain whenever someone says something I don't agree with I run from the conversation.

Credits

Poems by TJ Sykes
Illustrations by Webster Quoc Nguyen

Thanks to

Cici Jevae
for supporting me through the process.
Proof reading and editing.

Deandre Evans
for introducing me to R.A.W Talent and
being a real friend.

Donté Clark
for being a role model coming from a
community similar to mine.

Francisco Rojas
for supporting with the vision of this book.

Krista Midgette
for supporting with visual elements and composition

Molly Raynor
for listening and editing this poem, affirming
and encouraging me during my writing process.

Tina and Tim
for creating me and continuing to be my inspiration.

www.ingramcontent.com/pod-product-compliance
Lightning Source LLC
Chambersburg PA
CBHW022111160426
43198CB00008B/433